MW01166197

PRAYERS FOR THE JOURNEY

A DAILY COMPANION FOR THE WEARY, THE WAITING, AND THE WANDERING

Prayers for the Journey: A Daily Companion for the Weary, the Waiting, and the Wandering

© 2025 The Storehouse Group

Unless otherwise indicated, all Scripture quotations are taken from [Version, e.g., ESV, NIV].

Cover and illustrations © 2025 The Storehouse Group

Printed in the United States of America.

ISBN: 979-8-9985274-0-1

First Edition

FOREWORD

It was 2022. We had made it through the jarring years of 2020–2021—**but barely**.

I was breathing. Alive. But something inside me felt like it was slipping away. My family was walking through deep tragedy, and the crisis hadn't lifted. It hasn't even now.

My faith in Jesus hadn't wavered, but I had lost the words to pray.

My heart longed for communion with God, but my soul was too weary to speak. I wasn't sure what to do.

I grew up in the evangelical church, and I remain deeply grateful for that foundation. But as I've walked further with Jesus, I've come to treasure the gift of liturgy—especially in seasons when the ground seems to quake beneath your feet. It was during those early days of personal exhaustion and family crisis that a few dear friends handed me books and printouts—collections of prayers they had prayed when they didn't know what else to say.

The words were unfamiliar, but the presence I encountered was not. These were not new prayers. They were ancient, time-tested, prayed by saints for generations. And slowly, daily, faithfully—they began to strengthen my soul.

The prayers and scriptures shared with me became a way to express what my heart was aching to say, even when my mind couldn't form the words.

In the introduction to this book, you'll read:

"Prayer is not just a practice—it is a lifeline.

That has been true for me. Prayer became the daily act of showing up—sitting in silence, confessing, repenting, declaring, pleading, reflecting, remembering. Sometimes my only prayer was a whispered **"Help."** Sometimes it was one of the written prayers in these pages. Sometimes it was a guttural cry of honest lament, like something pulled from the Psalms.

My hope for you is simple:

That these prayers would become a lifeline for you too.

That you would meet the **Living God—right where you are.**

That in praying the words of others, **your own voice would reawaken.**

I hope you find strength in the mix of classic and modern liturgies. I hope new "psalms" of praise and lament flow from your pen into the blank pages at the back.

And above all, I hope you come to know—more deeply than ever before—**you are not alone.**

May you live in the fullness of God's love and blessing, both now and forevermore.

CHRIS OTTS

CONTENTS

MARKED BY GRATITUDE, SENT IN PEACE....70

FINDING YOUR VOICE 79

INTRODUCTION

Prayer is not just a practice—it is a lifeline. It steadies us in uncertainty, roots us in love, and orients us toward the presence of God in all things. If you are holding this book, there's a good chance you already know that prayer matters—but maybe you, like many of us, have discovered how hard it can be to pray when life feels overwhelming, dry, or disorienting.

This book was born in a season like that. A time when words felt hard to find, and when strength seemed to be leaking out slowly, quietly. The heart still longed for God—but the mouth didn't always know what to say. And in that place, written prayers—passed down by saints and shared by friends—became like a daily cup of water in the wilderness. Steady. Life-giving. Enough for the day.

There will be times in life when your own words will pour out easily in prayer. There will be other times when your voice will tremble, your soul will ache, or your thoughts will race, and you may not know where to begin. In those moments, liturgical prayers can be a gift. They don't replace your own words or intimacy with God— they give you a scaffold to stand on when everything else feels like shifting ground. They give you language when you feel lost. They can steady your soul with truth when emotion threatens to take over.

This book is here not to speak for you, but to walk with you. You are the one on the journey. You are the one learning to pray—not just with your words, but with your whole life. These prayers are simply companions for the road. They are here to help you rise and kneel, bless and lament, cry out and surrender, speak peace and receive grace.

You'll find ancient creeds and contemporary blessings. Prayers for mornings and midnights, peace and protection, strength and surrender. Some are short enough to whisper on a walk. Others are long enough to pray through slowly, line by line. They are arranged in a rhythm: from entering God's presence to crying out for mercy, anchoring in Christ's words, interceding for others, waiting in quiet, receiving grace, standing in spiritual authority, giving thanks, and finally being sent out in peace.

The goal is not to complete this book cover to cover. The goal is to engage with it in a way that helps **you** become the kind of person who talks to God honestly and listens attentively. Use it as a daily guide or a seasonal companion. Let it fill the space before bed or open the morning with clarity. Bring it into your family rhythms, your personal devotions, or your leadership of others. Let the prayers you find here become your own—until they start to awaken new prayers rising from within you.

You were made to know God. You were made to speak to Him. You were made to listen and to live in step with His Spirit. No matter how weary, uncertain, or silent you feel right now—prayer is still possible. You are not too far gone. You are not too late. And you are not alone. This journey belongs to you, and God will be with you in every step.

So...

Take a breath.

Pick a page.

Speak the words—even if you aren't sure, you believe them yet.

And trust that the Spirit is already interceding with groans too deep for words.

The journey is unfolding, and prayer is how we stay awake to it.

How to Use This Book

This book isn't meant to be read straight through like a novel—or kept on a shelf until a crisis hits. It's built for rhythm, for repetition, and for return. Think of it less like a manual and more like a companion—something you can come back to again and again as your days unfold.

You might begin each morning with a familiar prayer, letting the words shape your heart before you speak your own. Or you might turn to a section that meets you in the moment—when you're anxious, weary, grateful, or in need of mercy. Let the headings guide you, but feel free to ignore them, too. The Spirit often meets us in the places we least expect.

You can pray these words out loud or silently. You can write your own in the pages at the back. You can use this with your **family** around the table, with **friends** in a **small group**, or **in solitude** as a centering moment in your day. The goal isn't to get through all the prayers. The goal is to be drawn closer to God—to remember you're not alone, and to learn to speak with honesty, reverence, and hope.

There is no wrong way to begin. Just begin.

WELCOMING GOD'S PRESENCE

Opening Invocation

Heavenly Father, I come before You today with a heart open to Your presence.

Still my racing thoughts, quiet my anxious heart, and help me become aware of Your nearness.

Let this time of prayer be a sacred moment—where I remember who You are and who I am in You.

I welcome You, Lord. Come and meet with me now.

O Lord, open our lips,

And our mouth shall proclaim Your praise.

O God, make speed to save us,

O Lord, make haste to help us.

Glory be to the Father, and to the Son, and to the Holy Spirit,

As it was in the beginning, is now, and ever shall be, world without end.

Amen.

THE APOSTLES' CREED

I believe in God, the Father Almighty,

Creator of heaven and earth.

I believe in Jesus Christ, His only Son, our Lord.

He was conceived by the Holy Spirit and born of the virgin Mary.

He suffered under Pontius Pilate, was crucified, died, and was buried;

He descended to the dead.

On the third day He rose again.

He ascended into heaven and is seated at the right hand of the Father.

He will come again to judge the living and the dead.

I believe in the Holy Spirit, the holy catholic Church,

The communion of saints, the forgiveness of sins,

The resurrection of the body, and the life everlasting.

Amen.

To the Triune God

Eternal God,

Creator of heaven and earth,

Father, Son, and Holy Spirit:

Have mercy and hear our prayer.

Lord Jesus Christ,

Son of the Living God,

Have mercy and hear our prayer.

Spirit of the Living God,

Guide and awaken our hearts.

We come to You, not because we must,

But because we may—

To offer praise, to surrender ourselves,

And to receive all that You have for us today.

Amen.

Psalm 23

The Lord is my shepherd, I shall not want.

He makes me lie down in green pastures.

He leads me beside still waters.

He restores my soul.

He leads me in paths of righteousness for His name's sake.

Even though I walk through the valley of the shadow of death, I will fear no evil,

for You are with me; Your rod and Your staff, they comfort me.

You prepare a table before me in the presence of my enemies;

You anoint my head with oil; my cup overflows.

Surely goodness and mercy shall follow me all the days of my life,

and I shall dwell in the house of the Lord forever.

PSALM 91:1–2

He who dwells in the shelter of the Most High

will abide in the shadow of the Almighty.

I will say to the Lord, "My refuge and my fortress,

my God, in whom I trust."

Psalm 103:1–5

Bless the Lord, O my soul,

and all that is within me, bless His holy name!

Bless the Lord, O my soul,

and forget not all His benefits,

who forgives all your iniquity,

who heals all your diseases,

who redeems your life from the pit,

who crowns you with steadfast love and mercy,

who satisfies you with good

so that your youth is renewed like the eagle's.

RETURNING TO MERCY

CONFESSION OF SIN

Most merciful God,

I confess that I have sinned against You

In thought, word, and deed,

By what I have done,

And by what I have left undone.

I have not loved You with my whole heart.

I have not loved my neighbor as myself.

I am truly sorry and I humbly repent.

For the sake of Your Son Jesus Christ,

Have mercy on me and forgive me.

That I may delight in Your will,

And walk in Your ways,

To the glory of Your Name.

Amen.

PRAYER OF CONFESSION AND REPENTANCE

Lord Jesus, I acknowledge my sin and the ways I have turned from You.

I repent for the pride, fear, and rebellion in my heart.

I renounce every agreement I've made with lies or darkness.

Cleanse me from unrighteousness.

Restore my joy in salvation and renew my heart.

I turn to You with all that I am.

Lead me into truth, holiness, and life.

Amen.

Litany of Trust

(USED WITH PERMISSION – SISTERS OF LIFE)

From the belief that I have to earn Your love — Deliver me, Jesus.

From the fear that I am unlovable — Deliver me, Jesus.

From the false security that I have what it takes — Deliver me, Jesus.

From the fear that trusting You will leave me more destitute — Deliver me, Jesus.

From all suspicion of Your words and promises — Deliver me, Jesus.

From the rebellion against childlike dependency on You — Deliver me, Jesus.

From refusals and reluctances in accepting Your will — Deliver me, Jesus.

From anxiety about the future — Deliver me, Jesus.

From resentment or excessive preoccupation with the past — Deliver me, Jesus.

From restless self-seeking in the present moment — Deliver me, Jesus.

From disbelief in Your love and presence — Deliver me, Jesus.

From the fear of being asked to give more than I have — Deliver me, Jesus.

From the belief that my life has no meaning or worth — Deliver me, Jesus.

From the fear of what love demands — Deliver me, Jesus.

From discouragement — Deliver me, Jesus.

That You are continually holding me, sustaining me, loving me — Jesus, I trust in You.

That Your love goes deeper than my sins and failings, and transforms me — Jesus, I trust in You.

That not knowing what tomorrow brings is an invitation to lean on You — Jesus, I trust in You.

That You are with me in my suffering — Jesus, I trust in You.

That my suffering, united to Your own, will bear fruit in this life and the next — Jesus, I trust in You.

That You will not leave me orphan — Jesus, I trust in You.

That You are present in Your Church — Jesus, I trust in You.

That Your plan is better than anything else — Jesus, I trust in You.

That You always hear me and, in Your goodness, always respond to me — Jesus, I trust in You.

That You give me the grace to accept forgiveness and to forgive others — Jesus, I trust in You.

That You give me all the strength I need for what is asked — Jesus, I trust in You.

That my life is a gift — Jesus, I trust in You.

That You will teach me to trust You — Jesus, I trust in You.

That You are my Lord and my God — Jesus, I trust in You.

That I am Your beloved one — Jesus, I trust in You.

Amen.

PRAYER OF RENEWAL AND TRUST

Lord, I place my life back into Your hands today.

Renew my mind, refresh my spirit, and restore my strength.

Let me trust in You with my whole heart.

I yield control to You again—my thoughts, my time, my resources, my relationships.

Remind me that You are faithful and that I am safe in Your love.

Do a new work in me, Lord.

I receive Your mercy. I step forward in grace.

Amen.

Prayer for Mercy

Lord, have mercy.

Christ, have mercy.

Lord, have mercy.

In Your compassion, hear my cry.

Let the weight I carry be lifted by Your grace.

Let the darkness be scattered by Your light.

Let Your mercy meet me in this moment—

Softening what is hard, healing what is broken,

And restoring what has been lost.

I receive Your mercy now,

Not because I've earned it,

But because You are good. Amen.

THE LORD'S PRAYER

Our Father, who art in heaven,

hallowed be Thy name.

Thy kingdom come, Thy will be done,

on earth as it is in heaven.

Give us this day our daily bread,

and forgive us our trespasses,

as we forgive those who trespass against us.

And lead us not into temptation,

but deliver us from evil.

For Thine is the kingdom, and the power, and the glory,

forever and ever.

Amen.

PRAYER OF SURRENDER AND GLORY

ADAPTED FROM JOHN 17:1–5

Father,

I come to You in this moment,

Laying down my life again.

Be glorified in me—

Not for my sake, but so You may be seen and known.

You've given me life,

And I know that true life is found in knowing You—

The one true God—and Jesus, the one You sent.

Help me finish the work You've given me to do.

Let my life reflect Your goodness.

And when the journey is done,

Let me return to You,

To the place of glory and love that existed before the world began.

Amen.

Prayer of Protection and Purpose For Those Close to Me

ADAPTED FROM JOHN 17:6–19

Father,

Thank You for those You've entrusted to me—

Family, friends, mentors, spiritual companions.

They belong to You,

And You've allowed our lives to intersect for purpose.

I lift them to You now.

Protect them.

Guard their hearts from evil.

Keep them anchored in truth—

Your Word is truth.

I don't ask that You take them out of difficulty,

But that You keep them safe within it.

Set them apart for Your purposes.

Fill them with joy that cannot be stolen,

And courage that cannot be shaken.

Just as You sent Jesus, send them.

Let them walk in confidence, in love, and in light.

I bless them in Your name.

Amen.

PRAYER FOR UNITY AND GLORY FOR ALL BELIEVERS

ADAPTED JOHN 17:20–26

Father,

I pray for all who call on Your name—

For the Church around the world.

Make us one.

Let our love for one another reflect the love between You and the Son.

Unify us,

So that the world would believe.

Help us see Your glory—

Not just in heaven, but here on earth,

As we carry Your Spirit within us.

Let Your love dwell richly in us.

May we know that we are fully loved, fully forgiven,

And never alone.

Show us Your glory,

Fill us with Your joy,

And bring us near to Your heart.

Let the world know You sent Jesus—

And that He is still alive in us today.

Amen.

CRYING OUT IN FAITH

Petition and Intercession

Lord, I bring before You the needs weighing on my heart today.

You are the God who hears, the One who sees, the One who saves.

I ask for healing—physical, emotional, and spiritual.

I ask for wisdom in every decision, peace in every storm, and provision in every need.

I lift up my family, my friends, my community.

Let Your kingdom come in our lives.

Move in power and mercy.

Make a way where there seems to be no way.

Help me trust You, even when I cannot see the outcome.

I lay these requests at Your feet and believe You are at work.

Amen.

Prayer of Protection and Deliverance

Almighty God, be my shield and defender.

Surround me with Your presence and cover me with the blood of Jesus.

Break every chain of darkness and confusion.

Shut the mouth of the accuser.

Deliver me from fear, from distraction, from temptation.

Rescue those I love.

Let Your angels encamp around us.

No weapon formed against me shall prosper, for You are my refuge and my strong tower.

I declare freedom, healing, and victory in Jesus' name.

Amen.

GENERATIONAL BLESSING PRAYER

USED WITH PERMISSION – DR. ED LAYMANCE

Father, thank You for the generations before me.

I honor the legacy of faith passed down, even through brokenness.

Where there was blessing—let it increase.

Where there was pain—let it be healed.

I choose to bless my children and their children in Your name.

Let our family be rooted in Christ, established in truth, and filled with joy.

I speak life over future generations:

That they will know You,

Love You,

And walk in their calling.

May our home be a place of peace, purpose, and presence—for every generation to come.

Amen.

The Beatitudes

Blessed are the poor in spirit, for theirs is the kingdom of heaven.

Blessed are those who mourn, for they shall be comforted.

Blessed are the meek, for they shall inherit the earth.

Blessed are those who hunger and thirst for righteousness, for they shall be satisfied.

Blessed are the merciful, for they shall obtain mercy.

Blessed are the pure in heart, for they shall see God.

Blessed are the peacemakers, for they shall be called sons of God.

Blessed are those who are persecuted for righteousness' sake, for theirs is the kingdom of heaven.

Blessed are you when others revile you and persecute you and utter all kinds of evil against you falsely on My account.

Rejoice and be glad, for your reward is great in heaven.

Amen.

REMAINING WITH THE ONE WHO SEES

Resting in God's Presence

Jesus, I quiet my soul before You.

I let go of every distraction.

I breathe in Your peace.

I breathe out my anxiety.

I am not here to perform or produce—only to be with You.

Speak, Lord. Or be silent. I am still.

Let my spirit come into alignment with Yours.

Help me trust that You are near—even when the room feels quiet.

I receive Your presence. I rest in Your love.

Amen.

PRAYER TO THE CRUCIFIED CHRIST

Christ Jesus, crucified and risen,

You took my sin, my sorrow, and my shame.

You bore my wounds and carried my grief.

You conquered death and opened the way to life.

I kneel at the foot of Your cross.

I remember Your sacrifice.

Let me never take for granted what You have done.

Shape my life in the pattern of Your love.

Give me the courage to carry my cross and follow You.

Amen.

LITANY OF LOVE
USED WITH PERMISSION – SISTERS OF LIFE

From all eternity, O Lord,

You are.

Before the mountains were born,

You are.

From age to age,

You are.

From the depths of my sin,

You called me.

From the place of darkness,

You rescued me.

From the pit of despair,

You raised me.

With cords of compassion,

You drew me.

With mercy unending,

You covered me.

With everlasting love,

You claimed me.

Even when I ran,

You followed.

Even when I doubted,

You stayed.

Even when I forgot,

You remembered.

Your love endures.

Your mercy triumphs.

Your faithfulness never fails.

Jesus, my Lord,

You are love.

You are mercy.

You are life.

Take my heart,

Take my past,

Take my future.

Make me new,

Make me whole,

Make me Yours.

Amen.

CHRIST WITH ME

Christ above me, very God of very God

Christ below me, incarnate of the dust

Christ at my right hand in my strength

Christ at my left hand in my weakness

Christ before me when seen

Christ behind me when unseen

Christ all around me filling all things everywhere with himself

Grace For What Lies Ahead

SHEMA (DAILY AFFIRMATION)

Hear, O Israel: The Lord is our God, the Lord is one.

You shall love the Lord your God with all your heart, and with all your soul, and with all your might.

Let these words be upon your heart. Teach them diligently to your children.

Speak of them when you sit at home and when you walk along the road,

when you lie down and when you rise.

PRAYER FOR GRACE

God of all grace, Almighty and Everlasting Father,

I come in need—of patience, strength, and forgiveness. Fill my emptiness with Your presence.

Where I have grown weary,

restore me.

Where I have stumbled,

lift me.

Where I have feared,

reassure me.

I lean not on my own understanding but trust in You.

Be my portion today, O Lord.

Amen.

Prayer for Peace

Prince of Peace,

Let Your calm settle the storms in my heart.

Quiet the noise around me.

Steady my thoughts.

Help me live in the stillness of Your Spirit.

Where there is conflict—bring harmony.

Where there is stress—bring rest.

Let peace rule in my mind, my home, and my relationships.

Amen.

PRAYER OF ST. FRANCIS

Lord, make me an instrument of Your peace:

Where there is hatred, let me sow love;

Where there is injury, pardon;

Where there is doubt, faith;

Where there is despair, hope;

Where there is darkness, light;

And where there is sadness, joy.

O Divine Master,

Grant that I may not so much seek to be consoled as to console;

To be understood as to understand;

To be loved as to love.

For it is in giving that we receive;

It is in pardoning that we are pardoned;

And it is in dying that we are born to eternal life.

Amen.

Standing in Victory

Personal Surrender Prayer

Lord, I surrender all I am to You today.

Every thought, every ambition, every fear, every burden—I lay it down.

I release control.

I give You my past, present, and future.

Create in me a clean heart and renew a right spirit within me.

Help me to trust You more than I trust myself.

Your will, not mine.

Your ways, not mine.

Your name be glorified in me today.

Amen.

RESTORATION AND RENEWAL PRAYER

Father, I need Your renewing presence.

Where I am dry, pour out Your Spirit.

Where I am broken, bring healing.

Where I am weary, breathe life.

I release exhaustion and receive Your strength.

I let go of self-reliance and welcome Your help.

Restore my joy.

Renew my passion.

Awaken my soul to Your love.

Amen.

Authority and Protection Prayer

In the mighty name of Jesus,

I take authority over every lie, every scheme, every assignment of the enemy.

I declare that I am a child of God, redeemed and set apart.

No weapon formed against me shall prosper.

I place the cross of Christ between me and all darkness.

Let the light of truth expose every deception.

Let the name of Jesus silence every accuser.

Protect my mind, my body, my relationships, and my calling.

Your banner over me is love.

Amen.

Invocation of the Holy Spirit

Come, Holy Spirit.

Fill this place. Fill my heart.

Empower me with courage.

Guide me into truth.

Speak words I cannot hear on my own.

Intercede where I cannot pray.

Remind me of everything Jesus has said.

Set my soul on fire.

Lead me into deeper intimacy with the Father.

Come, Holy Spirit. I welcome You.

Amen.

Spiritual Armor and Angelic Protection

Heavenly Father, I put on the full armor of God today:

The belt of truth

The breastplate of righteousness

The shoes of peace

The shield of faith

The helmet of salvation

And the sword of the Spirit, which is Your Word.

Send Your angels to guard me in all my ways.

Let Your glory surround me as a shield.

Let no fear take root in me.

Let me walk in boldness, clothed in Christ and covered by grace.

Amen.

MARKED BY GRATITUDE, SENT IN PEACE

BLESSING OF THANKSGIVING & PROVISION

Father, thank You for every good and perfect gift.

You are the Source of all provision.

You've met my needs and exceeded my expectations.

I release fear and embrace gratitude.

I trust You to supply what's needed in every season.

Make me a vessel of generosity.

Let my life overflow with thanksgiving and praise.

Amen.

71

Blessing for Wisdom & Understanding

Lord, I ask for wisdom that comes from above—

pure, peace-loving, considerate, full of mercy and good fruit.

Help me see with spiritual eyes.

Give me understanding beyond my experience.

Let me lead with clarity, speak with discernment,

and walk in a way that reflects Your truth.

Amen.

BLESSING FOR PEACE (SHALOM)

May the peace of God—

wholeness, harmony, fullness—

rest upon you today.

May your thoughts be settled,

your heart be steady,

your spirit be at ease.

The Lord bless you with shalom in every part of your life.

Amen.

THE AARONIC BLESSING (NUMBERS 6:24–26)

The Lord bless you and keep you;

the Lord make His face to shine upon you and be gracious to you;

the Lord lift up His countenance upon you and give you peace.

Prayer of Thanksgiving

Lord, thank You for life today.

Thank You for breath in my lungs and purpose in my steps.

Thank You for grace undeserved and mercies new each morning.

Let my eyes be open to Your gifts.

Let my heart overflow with praise.

I give You thanks now and always.

Amen.

CONFESSION OF THE MYSTERY

Christ has died.

Christ is risen.

Christ will come again.

Final Blessing & Commitment

I go forward in faith—

anchored in love,

rooted in truth,

empowered by grace.

I choose to walk in light,

to live with purpose,

to serve with joy.

God before me, God behind me, God within me—
always.

Amen.

FINDING YOUR VOICE

GUIDE TO WRITING YOUR OWN PRAYERS

Writing your own prayers can be a powerful way to engage deeply with God and express your heart honestly and creatively. Here are a few simple prompts to help you begin:

START WITH REVERENCE
God, You are... (Name a truth about who God is: faithful, healer, shepherd, etc.)

EXPRESS GRATITUDE
Thank You for... (What has God done or provided recently?)

CONFESS HONESTLY
I confess that... (Name a sin, struggle, or place where you need God's grace.)

Lord, I ask for... (What do you need spiritually, emotionally, or practically?)

I believe that... (Declare a truth or promise from Scripture over your life.)

In Jesus' name, Amen.

Let these prompts guide your words—but don't be afraid to simply pour out your heart. God is near and listening.

About the Author

Prayers for the Journey was written and compiled by **The Storehouse Group**, *a nonprofit initiative committed to restoring hope, wholeness, and holy imagination through faith-rooted resources, support, and generosity. The Storehouse Group exists to serve those on the margins—offering spiritual formation tools, crisis grants, and practical care for individuals navigating seasons of pain, transition, or calling. Every resource created is birthed from a desire to pour out what has first been cultivated with God in secret.*

Proceeds from this book go directly to the mission of The Storehouse Group—supporting leaders in crisis, providing mental health resources to those in need, and equipping everyday disciples to live with grounded faith and enduring hope. When you purchase this book, you're not just receiving a companion for your journey—you're joining a movement to be a refuge for others in theirs.

Made in the USA
Columbia, SC
30 April 2025